THE LIFE OF DAVID

Passions Pursued

Catherine Schell

13 Discussions for Group Bible Study

Neighborhood Bible Studies Publishers
P.O. Box 222
56 Main Street
Dobbs Ferry, NY 10522
1-800-369-0307
email: nbstudies@aol.com
www.NeighborhoodBibleStudy.org

neighborhood bible studies

GROUP PARTICIPANTS

Name	Address	Phone Number

Scripture quotations, unless otherwise indicated, are taken from the HOLY BIBLE, NEW INTERNATIONAL VERSION®. Copyright © 1973, 1978, 1984 by International Bible Society. Used by permission of Zondervan Publishing House. All rights reserved.

All rights reserved. No part of this book may be reproduced or transmitted in any form or by any means, electronic or mechanical, including photocopying, recording, or any information storage and retrieval system without written permission from Neighborhood Bible Studies, P.O. Box 222, 56 Main Street, Dobbs Ferry, New York, 10522; 1-800-369-0307; nbstudies@aol.com.

Copyright © 2006 by Catherine Schell

ISBN 1-880266-54-7
Sixth printing November 2002
Printed in the United States of America
Cover photo by Russell and Lynn Hudson

Contents

How to Use this Discussion Guide	7
INTRODUCTION to The Life of David	11
Discussion 1 *1 Samuel 16* CALLED FROM OBSCURITY	12
Discussion 2 *1 Samuel 17* RISING TO THE CHALLENGE	17
Discussion 3 *1 Samuel 18;19* SUCCESSFUL, POPULAR, PERSECUTED	24
Discussion 4 *1 Samuel 21-23;* *2 Samuel 23:13-17* PURSUED AND PROTECTED	29
Discussion 5 *1 Samuel 24;25* RESTRAINT AND FURY	37
Discussion 6 *1 Samuel 26;27;30* THE FUGITIVE WARRIOR	43
Discussion 7 *2 Samuel 5;6* KING OVER JUDAH AND ISRAEL	50
Discussion 8 *2 Samuel 7* GOD'S SERVANT	56
Discussion 9 *2 Samuel 11* ADULTERY AND MURDER	61

Discussion 10 *2 Samuel 12:1-25; Psalm 51*
JUDGMENT **66**

Discussion 11 *2 Samuel 13;15;16;18*
REAPING CONSEQUENCES **72**

Discussion 12 *2 Samuel 24; 1 Chronicles 21;22;28*
JUDGMENT AND DELIVERANCE
PREPARATIONS FOR THE TEMPLE **79**

Discussion 13 *Psalm 71*
REVIEW OF THE LIFE OF DAVID **85**

WHAT SHOULD OUR GROUP STUDY NEXT? **90**

HOW TO USE THIS DISCUSSION GUIDE

This study guide uses the inductive approach to Bible study. *It will help you discover for yourself what the Bible says.* It will not give you prepackaged answers. *People remember most what they discover for themselves and what they express in their own words.* The study guide provides three kinds of questions:

1. What does the passage say? What are the facts?
2. What is the meaning of these facts?
3. How does this passage apply to your life?

- Observe the facts carefully before you interpret the meaning of your observations. Then apply the truths you have discovered to life today. Resist the temptation to skip the fact questions since we are not as observant as we think. Find the facts quickly so you can spend more time on their meaning and application.

- *The purpose of Bible study is not just to know more Bible truths, but to apply them.* Allow these truths to make a difference in how you think and act, in your attitudes and relationships, in the quality and direction of your life.

- Each discussion requires about one hour. Decide on the amount of time to add for socializing and prayer.

- *Share the leadership.* If a different person is the moderator or question-asker each week, interest grows and members feel the group belongs to everyone. The Bible is the authority in the group, not the question-asker.

- When a group grows to more than ten, the quiet people become quieter. Plan to grow and multiply. You can meet as two groups in the same house or begin another group so that more people can participate and benefit.

TOOLS FOR AN EFFECTIVE BIBLE STUDY

1. A study guide for each person in the group.

2. A modern translation of the Bible such as:
   NEW INTERNATIONAL VERSION (NIV)
   CONTEMPORARY ENGLISH VERSION (CEV)
   JERUSALEM BIBLE (JB)
   NEW AMERICAN STANDARD BIBLE (NASB)
   REVISED ENGLISH BIBLE (REB)
   NEW REVISED STANDARD VERSION (NRSV)

3. An English dictionary.

4. A map of the Lands of the Bible in a Bible or in the study guide.

5. Your conviction that the Bible is worth studying.

GUIDELINES FOR EFFECTIVE STUDY

1. Stick to the passage under discussion.

2. Avoid tangents. If the subject is not addressed in the passage, put it on hold until after the study.

3. Let the Bible speak for itself. Do not quote other authorities or rewrite it to say what you want it to say.

4. Apply the passage personally and honestly.

5. Listen to one another to sharpen your insights.

6. Prepare by reading the Bible passage and thinking through the questions during the week.

7. Begin and end on time.

How to Prepare A Study as Leader Or Participant

1. Begin your preparation early in the week. Pray for wisdom and the guidance of the Holy Spirit as you study.

2. Read the *background passages* indicated for each study, as well as the actual *discussion sections*. (Though the passages are long, they are narrative in style, interesting in content, and can be read quickly.) Then *reread* the sections for discussion.

3. As you read, make a chronological outline of the David's life. Note any experiences with God and with people that seem significant in the his development.

4. Consider David's family background and his social position in his culture.

5. Especially observe the development of the David's relationship with God.

6. The Eternal God has not changed. People have the same basic needs and many of the same problems that they did in Old Testament times. Watch for lessons you can learn from the life of David, his family, others involved with him, and their relationship to God.

7. Use the discussion questions and cross references provided by each lesson in this study guide. Think through the answers as you find them in the Bible passages. Since there are 13 discussions on the life of David, try to see one week's study in the context of the other studies on that man's life.

HELPS FOR THE QUESTION-ASKER

1. Prepare by reading the passage several times, using different translations if possible. Ask for God's help in understanding it. Consider how the questions might be answered. Observe which questions can be answered quickly and which may require more time.

2. Begin on time.

3. Lead the group in opening prayer or ask someone ahead of time to do so. Don't take anyone by surprise.

4. Ask for a different volunteer to read each Bible section. Read the question. Wait for an answer. Rephrase the question if necessary. Skip questions already answered by the discussion. Resist the temptation to answer the question yourself.

5. Encourage everyone to participate. Ask the group, "What do the rest of you think?" "What else could be added?"

6. Receive all answers warmly. If needed, ask, "In which verse did you find that?" "How does that fit with verse...?"

7. If a tangent arises, ask, "Do we find the answer to that here?" Or suggest, "Let's write that down and look for the information as we go along."

8. Discourage members who are too talkative by saying, "When I read the next question, let's hear from someone who hasn't spoken yet today."

9. Use the summary questions to bring the study to conclusion on time.

10. Close the study with prayer.

11. Decide on one person to be the host and another person to ask the questions at the next discussion.

INTRODUCTION *to the Life of David*

A thousand years after his ancestor Abram set out for the land of Canaan, a teenage shepherd-boy tended his father's flocks in the Judean countryside. The LORD who called Abram chooses David to be the shepherd of his people Israel, and later generations look back to his rule as Israel's golden age. A thousand years after David, the Gospel of Matthew records "the genealogy of Jesus Christ, the son of David, the son of Abraham."

The life of David is the most extensively covered single story in the Bible, and we know more about him than any other person in Scripture. The early Iron Age setting of David's life was a time of insecurity and change, influenced by Canaanite sexual immorality and the violence of Philistine border wars. In the midst of unfavorable human conditions surprisingly similar to our own day three millennia later, we watch the development and accomplishments of this gifted human being with a passionate heart for God.

These discussion studies provide the opportunity to immerse oneself in David's life and times. Take time each week to read the Bible passages that set the discussion sections in context before you study them using the guide questions. Begin your reading early in the week. As you move through the series of studies, keep brief notes on what you discover about David, his relationships with other people, and his personal relationship to God.

He [God] chose David his servant and took him from the sheep pens; from tending the sheep he brought him to be the shepherd of his people Jacob, of Israel his inheritance. And David shepherded them with integrity of heart; with skillful hands he led them. (Psalm 78:70-72)

DISCUSSION 1

Called From Obscurity

1 SAMUEL 16

The people of Israel have asked for a king to lead them, to go before them and fight their battles. Although by doing this they are rejecting the LORD as king, God directs the prophet Samuel to anoint Saul—from a respected family, young and handsome, standing head and shoulders above everyone else. If you were on an executive search for the first CEO for an emerging company, what would you think of Saul?

Presenting Saul to the assembled tribes of Israel as the man the LORD has chosen, the prophet carefully explains the rights and duties of kingship in Israel*. The LORD confirms Saul's appointment by sending the Spirit of God upon him in power, and uses him to deliver the people from their Ammonite enemies. Saul, however, begins to act independently of God's commands, and forgets that he serves under God as regent over the people. When he arrogantly rejects God's orders to completely destroy the Amalekites and their possessions, the LORD rejects Saul as king over Israel.

*SEE 1 SAMUEL 10:24, 25; DEUTERONOMY 17:14-20.

What characteristics would you include when describing an ideal national leader? An ideal spiritual leader?

To prepare this discussion, read 1 Samuel 8—13; 15; 16, to place David in the context of events that precede his anointing and reign. Study chapter 16 using the guide questions.

READ 1 SAMUEL 16:1-13

1. Describe this scene in which David is anointed by Samuel to be king. Look at these verses as you would to make a documentary film of the event.

Note: the word LORD *translates the name YHWH, meaning I AM WHO I AM, the Self-existent One), by which God made himself known to Israel. The* LORD *is the God of Abraham, Isaac, and Jacob, and is the name by which God is to be remembered forever (Exodus 3:15). YHWH was probably pronounced Yahweh.*

2. What does the LORD want Samuel to learn from this experience?

   Why doesn't God simply tell Samuel from the outset that David is the chosen one?

3. How does the way that the LORD evaluates human beings differ from the way you judge a person's qualifications for a responsible position?

4. What does this incident reveal about David and his family?

   What change takes place in David at this anointing?

5. David will face persecution and testing before he is established as king of Israel. How may this process of his selection and anointing be of help to David as he later experiences such challenges?

READ 1 SAMUEL 16:14-23

6. In contrast to David, what now happens to Saul (verse 14)?

7. What situation in Saul's life brings David into his service?

   If you were David, what would you think, and how would you feel about such an invitation?

8. How do the king's attendants describe what is happening to Saul?

9. What do you learn about David's reputation, his appearance and his abilities as he enters Saul's service?

   How does Saul feel toward David?

10. What are David's responsibilities in the royal court (verses 21, 23)?

SUMMARY

1. What circumstances bring sudden changes in David's life?

2. Imagine yourself as the young David as the startling events of this chapter unfold—playing your harp alone while you protect your father's sheep; called in from the fields to be anointed king as Samuel passes over your brothers; then sought out for Saul's court to serve as the king's musician. In what ways are you different at the end of chapter 16 from what you were at the beginning?

CONCLUSION

In the presence of David's brothers, the prophet Samuel has anointed David to be king. Though David is the youngest of Jesse's sons, **the LORD who looks at the heart** chooses him above all the others, and comes upon him in power. As the Spirit of the LORD departs from

Saul, the king asks for a talented harpist whose music can soothe his torment. In this way David is introduced to the royal court and comes to know King Saul.

PRAYER

O LORD, though you rule over all nations, you know each of us and our inmost thoughts, our desires and abilities. Three thousand years ago you called a young man from tending sheep to shepherd your people Israel. In your choice of David we learn you do not judge by outer appearance or age or birth order, but that you look at the heart.

Thank you for caring about us today as individuals, families, communities and nations. Grant us singleness of heart to care first for what pleases you. Help us to use the talents and skills you have given us for your glory, and the good of this world in which we live.

We pray in the name of the Great Shepherd of the sheep, our LORD Jesus Christ. Amen.

In preparation for Discussion 2, read 1 Samuel chapter 17. Then study the sections for discussion using the guide questions. Fill out the chart in question 10.

DISCUSSION 2

Rising to the Challenge

1 SAMUEL 17

Because Saul has shown himself to be the ruler of his people, the Spirit of the LORD has departed from Saul. In a private ceremony in the presence of his brothers the prophet Samuel has anointed David to be king and the Spirit of the LORD has come upon him in power. As Israel's Philistine enemies gather for war, Saul and the Israelites assemble to meet them.

You may have encountered a school or neighborhood bully during your childhood. You could choose to stand in defiance of the bully, cower in fear, or join the intimidator's support team. Such experiences prepare us for similar encounters with different stakes in adult life. Briefly describe an experience of bullying that you or someone you know has faced. How did you respond?

In preparation for this study, review what you discovered about David in the first discussion. Then study 1 Samuel 17 using the guide questions on the sections for discussion, and fill out the chart in question 10.

READ 1 SAMUEL 17:1-31

1. Why does David go to the battlefield, and what are his responsibilities there?

2. Describe the situation David discovers when he arrives (verses 2, 3, 20-24).

Note: Like earlier Egyptians and Canaanites and the Greeks, the Philistines sometimes used champion warfare in which chosen powerful men represented their respective armies. Combat between these two individuals determined which army was victorious.

3. What is the reaction of the men of Israel to Goliath's challenge?

   What reward is offered to any man who kills Goliath?

Note: A king could send out a champion rather than going himself. Even if a king were a great warrior, he would give other capable fighters the chance to prove their skills first. By this time (verse 16), Saul should have been willing to take up the challenge himself.

4. How does David's view of the situation (verse 26) differ from that of the other Israelites?

Note: **Uncircumcised Philistine**-*Circumcision was **a sign of the covenant** between God and Abraham (Genesis 17: 1—14) to whom the* LORD, *God Almighty, had promised the land on which the Philistine was standing.*

> What history does David remember that Saul and his people have forgotten? See 1 Samuel 11:11,13; 12:6, 7, 20-22.

5. Instead of the rewards offered for killing the Philistine, what motivates David to take Goliath's challenge?

> What difference would it make in your life if you were to embrace the same motivation as David?

6. When he hears David's comments, what is his oldest brother Eliab's response?

> From David's reply to Eliab's angry comments, what do you learn about the relationship between David and his older brothers?

READ 1 SAMUEL 17:32-54

7. David's questions are overheard and his concern reported to Saul. What do you learn about David's courage and his faith in the living God from his interview with Saul?

What past experiences give David such confidence (verses 34–37)?

8. What present opportunities do you have to trust God so that you may be prepared to face more difficult situations in days ahead?

9. What protection does David refuse? Why?

What does David recognize as his real security? See also Psalm 118:6, 8, 9.

10. Evaluate the two champions facing each other:

	Goliath	**David**
Physical Description	(vv. 4, 33)	(vv. 33, 42)
Personal Attitude	(vv. 10, 42, 43)	(v. 37, 46)
Armor	(vv. 5, 6, 41)	(vv. 38, 39)
Weapons	(v. 7)	(v. 40)
Verbal Challenge	(vv. 43, 44)	(vv. 45–47)

Imagine yourself as a young Israelite soldier later describing to his family the long standoff between the Israelites and the Philistines (17:16, 21-25). Referring to notes in this chart, describe the two champions as they now confront each other.

11. How does David meet Goliath's threats and mocking?

    What does David believe that his victory will reveal?

    Restate verse 47 in modern terms.

12. What does David recognize about himself?

    about the LORD?

Note: The sling was an effective weapon in skilled hands (Judges 20:16), and Goliath would have been aware of its use in organized warfare. A skilled slinger could hurl a round stone weighing a pound or more a hundred yards at the speed of one hundred miles an hour.

13. Imagining yourself again as a young Israelite soldier talking later to his family, describe the one-round fight between David and Goliath (verses 48-51).

How does the unexpected death of their champion affect the Philistines?

SUMMARY

1. From this chapter, what sort of person do you find David to be?

2. What is the secret of his success in the contest with Goliath?

3. What "giant" are you facing in your life right now? Or, relate a past experience in which God helped you to overcome a "giant".

CONCLUSION

David's faith in the LORD, his desire to see God honored and the reproach against Israel removed, have enabled him to face and destroy Goliath. When the Philistine giant strides out to face David, he expects another sort of battle. To his peril, Goliath discounts David's abilities and his confidence in the power of the living God of Israel. Instead of becoming servants to the Philistines*, the troops of Israel and Judah heartened and energized by David's success, chase the Philistine invaders back to their own cities.

PRAYER

Almighty LORD, *in whose name David confronted Goliath, as we face the giants in our lives, remind us that the battle is yours. Grant us the perspective and the confidence that David had—that we are not saved by human skills and weapons, but by your power. We ask these things that your glory may be seen through our lives today. Amen.*

*The Philistines were descendants of Sea Peoples who had migrated from the region of the Aegean Sea 200 years before David's time. The Sea Peoples are thought to be the ones responsible for the fall of the great Hittite empire and the destruction of many cities along the Mediterranean coast of Syria and Palestine. Driven back from their attacks on Egypt, they established five capital cities (Ashkelon, Ashdod, Ekron, Gath, Gaza) on the southern coast of Palestine and were always trying to expand their territory into Israelite areas. The Philistines were a continuing threat to the Israelites during the reign of Saul.

In preparation for the next discussion, read chapters 18 and 19 of 1 Samuel in at least two different translations. Then study these chapters using the guide questions.

DISCUSSION 3

Successful, Popular, Persecuted

1 SAMUEL 18; 19

David's confidence in the living God, the LORD Almighty (17:26, 45-47), has been vindicated. His victory over the champion Goliath has resulted in the flight of the Philistine armies back to their own territory, routed by the pursuing Israelites. The Israelite commander immediately brings David, still holding the Philistine's head, to King Saul for an interview. What Saul's son Jonathan hears greatly impresses this heir-apparent to the throne of Israel (17:57, 58; 18:1).

How do you respond to the successes of others? To your own successes?

When you prepare this discussion, review what you learned about David in the first two discussions. Then read 1 Samuel 18 and 19 in two different translations before studying these chapters using the guide questions.

READ 1 SAMUEL 18:1-30

1. How does Jonathan react to David (verse 1)?
2. In what specific ways does Jonathan express his regard for David?

*Note: The word for the **robe** that Jonathan was wearing (verse 4) often referred to a royal robe. **Tunic, sword, bow** and **belt** were a warrior's equipment. Only King Saul and Jonathan had swords on the day of the battle in 13:22.*

3. What begins Saul's jealousy of David (verse 8)?

   How serious a threat does King Saul consider David's popularity?

4. What is happening to Saul?

   Why does he fear David (15:26; 18:12-16, 28, 29)?

   Through all of this, what do you learn about David?

*Note: (verse 18) **an evil spirit from God** (also 16:14) – Saul's disobedience is punished by the attacks of an evil spirit. It seems also to be used here for the negative spiritual influence that produces such results as suspicion, paranoia, shortsightedness and indecision, in contrast to the courage, confidence, wisdom and insight that Saul demonstrated earlier. Saul's loss of God's Spirit upon him and his anxious state of mind open the way for David's introduction as harpist to the royal court.*

5. As you trace the shifting changes in Saul's feelings toward David throughout this chapter, list the different words and phrases that describe these feelings.

   What danger is there in nurturing such feelings?

6. What various actions (verses 10-25) does Saul take because of his fear and jealousy?

   What does the king intend by his actions toward David?

7. Though Saul increasingly fears David, what does the love of Saul's children for David (verses 1, 20, 28) tell you about how *they* view his intentions and motives?

READ 1 SAMUEL 19:1-18

8. When Saul orders his attendants and his son to kill David, what actions does Jonathan take to protect his friend?

9. Observe Jonathan's wise reasoning as he seeks to reconcile the king and David (verses 1-7). How successful is he?

10. What occasions the renewal of Saul's jealousy?

If you are a Christian, what can you do about jealousy if it rises up in your heart (Colossians 3:1-3, 8, 12, 13)?

11. By what means does David escape Saul's plot against his life in verses 11-18?

SUMMARY

1. From this study and what you discovered in Discussions 1 and 2, what sort of person do you find David to be?

    In what particular areas do you think David's strength lies?

2. What temptations are peculiar to the experience of sudden success and popularity, or of someone's irrational jealousy?

    What have you learned from David's life to help you in such situations?

3. What help does David say that the LORD offers at such times?
    Psalm 27:1, 5
    Psalm 40:1-3
    Psalm 103:1-6, 15-18

CONCLUSION

While still in his youth David rises swiftly from obscurity to great fame in Israel, but because of King Saul's jealousy he soon finds himself in danger of his life. David's faith in God and his desire to see the LORD's people victorious enabled him to face Goliath. As the object of the king's increasing fear and envy, David's faith is tested by new dangers.

PRAYER

LORD God, cleanse our hearts from jealousies and proud ambition for ourselves and for our loved ones. Help us to walk in the simplicity of a faith that learns to trust you and desires to please you, through all the changing circumstances of our lives. Grant that we find contentment not in position, popularity or success, but in the awareness of your love for us in our LORD Jesus Christ. Amen.

To prepare for the next discussion, review what you have learned to this point about David—his character, his abilities and his faith in God. Then read 1 Samuel, chapters 20—23, and study the discussion sections using the guide questions.

DISCUSSION 4

Pursued and Protected

1 SAMUEL 21-23; 2 SAMUEL 23:13-17

David is now convinced it is no longer possible to be reconciled with the king. Warned by Jonathan that Saul is determined to kill him, David goes to the tabernacle at Nob to seek God's guidance through Ahimelech the priest (22:10a, 14, 15a). The suddenness of his departure has caught David unarmed and without adequate provisions.

Reflect on an experience in which you found yourself in danger. How did you respond to the situation?

Review briefly what you learned in the first three discussions about David's character, his abilities and his faith in God. In preparing this study, read the full text of 1 Samuel, chapters 20—23, before you study the discussion sections using the guide questions.

READ 1 SAMUEL 21:1-9; 22:9, 10

1. Describe the situation David encounters when he goes to Ahimelech the priest.

Note: It is not clear why David deceives Ahimelech as to why he comes alone. Perhaps he resorts to deceit because he fails to trust God to deliver him this time. If David is trying to protect the priest from being involved in his escape from the king, he is not successful.

When David declares that he and his men are ceremonially clean, what provisions does he obtain from Ahimelech?

*Note: 21:6—**the holy (consecrated) bread, Bread of the Presence**, a thank offering symbolizing God's provision of daily bread for his people. Twelve loaves, one for each tribe, were placed weekly before God on a table in the Holy Place in the tabernacle. Only the priests were to eat the old bread (Exodus 25:30; Leviticus 24:5-9). Jesus referred to this incident in Matthew 12:1-4.*

READ 1 SAMUEL 21:10-15; 22:1

2. Even though Gath is the town from which Goliath came, David may count on the possibility that the King of Gath will accept him as a well-known warrior fleeing from Saul, and welcome him to fight *with* the Philistines instead of *against* them. What works against any such plan (verse 21:11)?

3. When he becomes **very much afraid of Achish** (verse 12), what does David do to convince the Philistine ruler that he is no danger to Achish and his forces? How well does his ruse succeed?

Note: In the Near East of that day, insane people were sometimes accepted as messengers of the gods and allowed to live, though often excluded from ordinary society.

READ 1 SAMUEL 22:1, 2

4. What types of people gather around David in the stronghold of Adullam?

   Why are these four hundred men drawn to David? Compare with Matthew 9:10-13.

   Would you choose to follow David at this point in his career? Why, or why not?

Note: Adullam, about 16 miles southwest of Jerusalem, was in a kind of "no man's land" between Israelite and Philistine territory.

5. How would the experience of leading such men prepare David to rule the kingdom?

   What sympathies would he learn?

READ 2 SAMUEL 23:13-17 *(an incident from the same period as 1 Samuel 22 and 23)*

6. What does this incident reveal about David's relationship with his men?

   What value does David place on the water from Bethlehem's well?

   Whom does David recognize as the only one worthy of such a gift?

7. Compare yourself with David's chief men. How do you rate as a follower of the LORD Jesus Christ, a far greater leader than David?

   What have you dared for the LORD?

1 Samuel 22:3-21—David requests safe haven for his parents with the King of Moab, out of Saul's reach. On the prophet Gad's instructions, David leaves his desert stronghold for the forest of Heresh in the tribal territory of Judah. When King Saul learns that David and his men have been discovered, he interrogates and threatens his officials, questioning their loyalty. Doeg reports David's visit to Nob. Infuriated that anyone would help his enemy, Saul orders the death of all the priests and their families, and the destruction of their possessions. When Saul's own guards refuse to commit this outrageous

sacrilege, only the Edomite Doeg carries out Saul's orders. The lone survivor, Abiathar, a son of Ahimelech, escapes to David and reports the massacre. Hearing the news, David holds himself responsible for all the deaths at Nob, and promises Abiathar the priest that he will be safe with him.

READ 1 SAMUEL 23:1-6

8. What report from Keilah moves David to consider an attack against the Philistines?

   With Abiathar the priest now in his company, what advantage does David have over Saul (verses 2, 4, 6)?

*Note: The **ephod** was a sleeveless vestment worn by the high priest. Attached to it was the breastpiece in which were placed sacred lots (**Urim** and **Thummim**), ordained as the means to determine the guidance of God.*

9. What happens when David and his men act on faith in God's promise to give them the Philistines?

READ 1 SAMUEL 23: 7-14

10. When David learns what Saul is plotting against him, how does he address God, and what information does he gain?

11. Rather than subjecting Keilah to a destructive siege by Saul, what does David do (verses 13, 14)?

Contrary to what Saul says in verse 7 about David, what proves to be true in David's experience (verse 14)?

Note: The Wilderness (Desert) of Ziph (NRSV, NIV) in the tribal territory of Judah, about 13 miles southeast of Keilah, was a sparsely inhabited hilly area in which David and his growing fugitive band could safely hide. Horesh, meaning a wooded height, was in the Judean wilderness.

READ 1 SAMUEL 23:15-18

12. For a long time, David has faced constant danger from Saul's unrelenting pursuit, and the wearying insecurity of continual movement in wilderness places. Imagine yourself in David's shoes. What would Jonathan's visit and his confident declaration about the future mean to David at this point?

1 Samuel 23:19-29—While closing in on David and his men in the Desert of Maon, Saul receives news of a Philistine raid that requires his immediate attention. Delivered from his enemy for the moment, David moves to En Gedi, an oasis with a continual water source and many nearby caves, halfway down the Dead Sea, about 35 miles southeast of Jerusalem.

SUMMARY

1. What pressures does David face in the situations he encounters in chapters 21—23?

2. Imagine yourself in one of those situations. What do you learn from David about how, or perhaps how not, to deal with a situation producing great stress in your own life?

3. Is there a situation in which you can play Jonathan's part in helping a friend to find strength in God?

CONCLUSION

David faces a series of desperate situations:
- sudden flight to escape King Saul's determination to kill him
- feigning insanity to escape the Philistines at Gath
- Doeg's massacre of 85 priests and their families after Ahimelech helps David
- Saul's plan to besiege Keilah to capture David and his men after they deliver the town from the Philistines
- the Ziphites' intention to help Saul track down David and his men.

In these events, David reveals his desire to know and do the will of God, wise provision for the safety of his parents, and the ability to lead a band of 400 men with skill, determination and courage, inspiring their deep personal loyalty in dangerous circumstances.

PRAYER

O LORD, God of truth, I take refuge in you. Hear my prayer. Be my foundation, my rock of refuge, my strong fortress. I place myself in your hands for you have redeemed me, and I trust in you. All the circumstances of my life are in your hands. Guide me and protect me as you did your servant David, for your own name's sake. Amen.

To prepare for Discussion 5, review what you have learned about David to this point. Then read the full text of 1 Samuel 24 and 25, before studying these chapters using the guide questions.

DISCUSSION 5

Restraint and Fury

1 SAMUEL 24;25

Saul's unreasoning fear of conspiracy has led to the death of 85 priests and their families because Ahimelech inquired of the LORD for David and gave him provisions. Abiathar who alone survived the massacre has joined David's growing company of four hundred men. He brings with him the priestly ephod by which he can obtain God's guidance for David. Saul no longer has access to such guidance, and continues to pursue David, intent on killing him. When the king suddenly interrupts his pursuit in order to deal with a Philistine raid against Israel, David escapes to **En Gedi,** an oasis with a continual water source and many nearby caves.

What impact has revenge, or resisting the urge to seek revenge, had on your life?

In preparing for this discussion, review David's recent experiences in 1 Samuel 20—23. Then study chapters 24 and 25 using the guide questions.

READ 1 SAMUEL 24

1. Although Saul pursues David with three thousand chosen men, what opportunity comes to David to destroy him?

2. Even when his men urge David to treat Saul as an enemy, what does his choice to protect him reveal about how he views Saul as king?

3. Saul's robe would have a distinctive design or stitching to mark him out as king. What argument with physical evidence to prove it, does David use when he confronts the king?

   For what does David pray (verses 12, 15)?

4. What poignant response does the king make to David's arguments, and what does he foresee?

5. Why is David able to be so generous toward King Saul?

   How does this incident help to fit David to lead the nation?

6. Compared with David, how do you act when given an opportunity for revenge?

READ 1 SAMUEL 25

7. Why might David expect favorable treatment from Nabal (verses 7, 8, 15, 16)??

   Describe Nabal and his reactions to the courteous request from David's young men.

8. What does his reaction (verses 13, 21,22) to Nabal's insulting refusal tell you about David?

   What further insight does that reaction give you about David's very different attitude toward Saul (24:4-6)?

9. What sort of person is Abigail?

   Why would she keep her actions (verses 18, 19) from her husband?

10. What reasons does Abigail give David that he should forgo his plan of vengeance against Nabal (verses 24-27)?

What future does Abigail foresee for David (verses 28-31)?

11. Why does David give thanks to the LORD and to Abigail?

    How does David evaluate what has happened?

    Why is it wrong to avenge ourselves, even when we have been wronged? (Romans 12:19, 21; James 1:19, 20)

12. What does David conclude when he hears the news of Nabal's death?

    What sort of influence do you think that a woman like Abigail would have on David as his wife?

Note: Verses 40, 43, 44—These marriages before David becomes king are made to strengthen his political ties and economic position.

SUMMARY

1. How do you account for the apparently contradictory ways in which David reacts in the two major incidents in today's study?

2. What evidence of David's humility do you see in these chapters?

What ultimately rules his decisions?

Conclusion

David rejects the tempting opportunity to kill King Saul and take the kingdom that God has promised will be his. David is patient in the face of Saul's continued provocation, and he accepts Abigail's wise counsel not to avenge himself against Nabal. His patience is grounded in his understanding of the righteousness and faithfulness of God. David continues to trust the LORD to work out the circumstances of his future to give him the kingdom at the appointed time.

Prayer

Gracious God, Preserver and Sustainer of all who depend on you, help us like your servant David to trust you in good times and bad. Keep us from taking matters into our own hands when we should wait for your deliverance. Grant us courage to believe that your will is perfect, that your truth will prevail. Forgive us that we so quickly forget the lessons of the past. Help us to forgive the sins of others against us as you have forgiven us in your Son, Jesus Christ. Amen

In preparation for Discussion 6, read 1 Samuel 26:1—28:2; 29; 30; 1 Chronicles 12:1-22. Then study the sections for discussion using the guide questions.

DISCUSSION 6

The Fugitive Warrior

1 SAMUEL 26; 27; 30

Pursued by Saul and his forces in the Desert of Engedi, David unexpectedly had an opportunity to kill the king. He refused to do this, believing the kingship of Israel to be the LORD's to give, and David would not seize it. In contrast to his restraint toward Saul, David reacted in fury to Nabal's insulting refusal to honor his men's protection of Nabal's shepherds and flocks. Only Abigail's wise intervention restrained David from bloody vengeance. When her husband dies soon after, struck down by the LORD, David asks Abigail to become his wife.

On what principles or persons do you rely when you face a troubling dilemma?

After you review briefly what you have learned about David in previous discussions, read the full text of 1 Samuel 26; 27:1—28:2; 29; 30. For additional information on David's forces at Ziklag, read 1 Chronicles 12:1-22. Then study through the sections for discussion using the guide questions.

READ 1 SAMUEL 26:1-12

1. Why does Saul begin to pursue David again?

   What do you learn about David's courage and abilities in verses 4-7?

2. What does David demonstrate by how he responds to Abishai's tempting offer?

   What reasons does David give (verses 9-11)?

   What standard controls your ambitions for yourself and for your children?

READ 1 SAMUEL 26:13-25

3. In talking to Saul, what two possibilities does David suggest for Saul's enmity toward him (verse 19)?

4. How does Saul respond to David's argument and plea? What does the king admit?

READ 1 SAMUEL 27:1-4

5. In spite of all Saul's claims and confessions, what does David now realize about him?

What does David do that causes Saul to stop searching for him?

6. What is the size of David's company as they move to Gath?

1 Samuel 27:5—28:2; 29—-By seeking sanctuary in Gath, David is offering his band as mercenary troops to Achish the King of Gath. (Mercenary soldiers, fairly common in the world of that day, were often political refugees who hated the regime that had caused their exile.) Knowing the enmity between King Saul and David, Achish believes David will be loyal to him as Saul's enemy and grants him sanctuary.

David's new location in Ziklag south of Gath gives him opportunity to launch raids further south to eliminate some of Israel's enemies on its borders, and he leaves no survivors to inform the Philistines. Plunder from these raids supports David's men, and he leads Achish to believe that he is raiding outlying Israelite areas.

David is obligated to serve Achish when called for any military ventures. As the Philistines gather forces for an impending battle against Israel, he is rescued from the dilemma of having to fight against his own people. Other Philistine commanders question David's loyalty in such a battle, so Achish sends David and his men back to Ziklag.

READ 1 SAMUEL 30:1-6

7. Describe in detail the situation they find when David and his men return to their home base at Ziklag.

8. How do David and his men react to the devastation they see (verses 4-6)?

9. Beyond his own personal losses, what added pressure does David face?

    How does David handle this?

READ 1 SAMUEL 30:7-20

10. What do you learn about David from what he does before any possible pursuit of the raiders?

    How can David's example here help you in facing a disastrous situation?

11. Without any rest after their three-day journey back to Ziklag, a third of David's band is too exhausted to continue pursuing the raiders. When the pursuers encounter an abandoned Egyptian slave, what strategic intelligence do they gain when they show him kindness?

12. How complete is the rescue the four hundred men accomplish?

READ 1 SAMUEL 30:21-31

13. On what basis does David reject the urging of the troublemakers and evil men in his victorious band (verses 22, 23)?

What does David's decision (verses 24, 25) reveal about him as a person and as a leader?

Note: Verses 26-30— Some towns in Judah have helped David's band of men in their years of wandering. His generosity in sending gifts of Amalekite plunder to the elders of these towns has political implications. David can expect them to back him in asserting his kingship whenever Saul dies.

SUMMARY

1. In the events in this study, what have you learned about David from:
    - his actions entering and leaving Saul's encampment
    - his argument before King Saul
    - his flight into sanctuary in Philistine territory
    - his deception of Achish
    - his men's treatment of the Egyptian slave
    - his decision about how to treat the soldiers who stayed with the supplies

2. Which aspect of David's character do you most want to develop in yourself at this time in your life?

Conclusion

Still patient in the face of Saul's continuing provocation, David resists the temptation of a second opportunity to kill King Saul. He continues to trust God to work out the circumstances of his future and to give him the kingdom at the proper time. At Ziklag in Philistine territory, when his soldiers threaten mutiny because of the bitter loss of their families and possessions, David finds strength in the LORD his God. Avoiding precipitate action, he asks for and follows directions from the LORD. When he leads his soldiers in successful rescue and recovery, David insists it is the LORD who has protected them and given them the victory. Therefore, all must share in what God has given them.

Prayer

LORD God, we can scarcely imagine the weariness, pain and discouragement that David and his men experienced in the long months they were hounded by Saul and his warriors. We sense the insecurity they must have felt in Philistine territory. As we imagine what it must be like to lead a group in such conditions, help us to persevere in faith as your servant David did. When we face disastrous loss, we ask you to strengthen us as you strengthened David. In situations that tempt us to bitterness of spirit, remind us that you are with us and you will never leave us. Give us a loving sensitivity toward others who are going through such times. May you be honored by our lives as we learn to trust you. For your glory and our good, we pray. Amen.

For the transition from Saul's rule to David's rule, read 1 Samuel 31 and 2 Samuel 1—4 in preparation for Discussion 7. To learn about the beginning of David's rule over Judah and Israel in a newly united kingdom, read 2 Samuel 5—7, and 1 Chronicles 12:23-40. Then study the discussion sections using the guide questions.

DISCUSSION 7

King over Judah and Israel

2 SAMUEL 5,6

While David and his men were rescuing families from Amalekite raiders in the south, the Philistines defeated the Israelite army in the north, and King Saul and his three sons died the same day. To begin to appreciate David's grief at their deaths, read aloud the lament he composed to mourn and honor Saul and Jonathan (2 Samuel 1:19-27). Perhaps you have experienced grief similar to David's? Someone may wish to comment here briefly.

As background for this discussion, read 1 Samuel 31; 2 Samuel 1—6; 1 Chronicles 11:1-9; 12:23—13:14; 15:1—16:6. Then study 2 Samuel 5 and 6, using the guide questions.

READ 2 SAMUEL 5:1-13

1. What reasons do the tribes of Israel give for asking David, already king over Judah, to be their king?

What specific legal arrangement do the elders of Israel make with him?

How long is David's reign?

Note: **Judah** *(verse 5) includes the tribes of Judah, Benjamin, and here likely also the tribe of Simeon.* **Israel** *(verse 1) refers to all the other tribes. Use a map in your Bible or Bible atlas to locate the areas of the different tribes.*

2. List everything you observe about Jerusalem, and about David, from verses 6-11.

Up to this time, Jerusalem has never been occupied by the Israelites. How does it become **the city of David**?

3. When the king of Tyre recognizes David as king over Israel and builds a palace for him, what does David know (perceive) at that point (verses 11, 12)?

Note: Verse 13—Royal marriages were a tool of diplomacy throughout the ancient Near East. This series of marriages strengthened David's economic and political position.

READ 2 SAMUEL 5:17-25

4. Hearing that David has been anointed king over Israel, the Philistines recognize he is a threat to their control in the north. Describe the Philistines' approach (verses 18, 22).

5. What do you learn about David as a warrior and as a servant of the LORD from how he reacts when the Philistines enter the land?

In dangerous situations requiring action in your own life what wise examples do David's actions here set for you?

Note: The series of military victories that the LORD gives David in Chapter 8 likely occur between chapters 5 and 6 (chapters placed together because they deal with the ark of God).

READ 2 SAMUEL 6:1-11

David recognizes how significant the ark of God is as the earthly throne of the God of Israel. As God's king over Israel, David intends to have the ark brought to Jerusalem from where it has been in Judah during the reign of Saul.

Note: The ark of God, the ark of the covenant of the LORD Almighty, was a wooden box about four feet long, two feet high and two feet wide, overlaid inside and out with sheets of gold, and open at the top. Four gold covered rings were attached to the sides to hold two poles used to carry the ark. A golden cover decorated with two winged cherubim sealed the ark that contained reminders of God's presence and action among them: the tablets of stone Moses gave to the people from Sinai, a jar of manna from their wanderings in the wilderness, and Aaron's rod that budded at the time of their deliverance from Egypt.

6. Describe the size, makeup and atmosphere of the procession accompanying the ark of God to Jerusalem (verses 1-5). What do you see and hear?

7. God's instructions through Moses on how the ark should be transported are not followed. By bringing the ark of God on an oxcart instead of on the shoulders of the Levites, what catastrophe disrupts the celebration?

   Why do you think David reacts as he does here (verses 7-9)?

Note: For David's later understanding of what happened here, see Numbers 4:15; 1 Chronicles 15:1, 2, 13 – 15.

READ 2 SAMUEL 6:12-23

8. Imagine you are filming the procession three months later as David brings the ark to Jerusalem (verses 12-19; 1 Chronicles 15:25-28). What do you see, hear, smell and taste?

9. How would you have reacted to it all, including David's participation in the event?

10. What do you learn about David's passionate attitude toward God from his participation in this joyous celebration, and from the ensuing breach between him and his wife Michal (verses 16, 20-22)?

SUMMARY

1. What events in chapter 5 confirm to David that the LORD's time has come for him to be established as king?

2. What lessons do you learn from the events in chapters 5 and 6 that can apply to your own life in our troubled time, nearly three thousand years after David?

3. Compare your spiritual life to David's attitude toward God in these two chapters.

CONCLUSION

Saul's kingdom has ended. David's years of living in the Judean wilderness are over. He has conquered the fortress of the Jebusites, strategically situated between the tribes of Israel to the north and Judah to the south. Taking up residence there, he makes Jerusalem the City of David, his royal city, the capital of the whole kingdom. In bringing the ark of God to Jerusalem, David acknowledges God's kingly rule over him and over his people whom he is to serve as their shepherd.

PRAYER

LORD God, your servant David puts us to shame. Even after many years as a warrior, he doesn't depend on his past experiences for wisdom, but seeks your guidance in new battles with his enemies. Thank you for bringing David at long last to rule over your people. Compared to David's passionate responses to you in celebrating your deliverance and your rule, we are often inhibited, insecure, proud, afraid to be different. Help us recognize what truly honors you. Amen.

To prepare for Discussion 8, read aloud from 2 Samuel, Chapter 7:
- **the conversation between David and Nathan**
- **the word of the LORD through Nathan to David**
- **David's response in prayer as he sits before the LORD**

Try to put yourself in the shoes of David and of Nathan each time.

DISCUSSION 8

God's Servant

2 SAMUEL 7

Upon the death of King Saul, David at the age of thirty began to reign over his own tribe of Judah in Hebron. Seven and one-half years later, representatives of the northern tribes of Israel entered into a compact with David, recognizing him as their king also. David and his men have conquered the natural fortress of the Jebusites strategically situated on the border between Israel and Judah, enabling him to locate the capital of the newly united kingdom in Jerusalem. After a false start, the ark of the LORD has been installed in Jerusalem with great rejoicing among the people. David's exuberant participation in this joyous celebration has alienated his wife Michal.

In Discussion 1 you were asked what characteristics you would include when describing an ideal national leader and an ideal spiritual leader. Which, if any, of these characteristics have you observed to this point in David?

In preparation for today's discussion, review briefly what you learned about David in chapters 5 and 6. Then study chapter 7 using the guide questions.

Read 2 Samuel 7:1-17

1. According to verses 1-3, what kind of relationship exists between David and Nathan?

   When peace comes, to what do David's thoughts turn?

   What plans and ideas occupy your thought during leisure hours?

2. When the LORD reveals his plans to Nathan, how do they differ from David's plan that Nathan has approved?

   Of what does the LORD remind David about his dwelling-place in Israel in times past?

3. What does the LORD say about his past dealings with David?

   In verses 5, 8, God calls David *my servant* and *prince (ruler) over my people Israel*.

   What meanings do these titles convey?

4. For New Testament understanding of verses 13, 16, read Luke 1:31-33; Mark 11:7-10.

READ 2 SAMUEL 7:18-29

5. What does David do in response to this message from the LORD?

   In what ways may a person react when God says *no*?

6. In David's prayer, what are the specific items of praise? of petition?

   On what does David base these petitions?

7. What would David's recollection of God's past faithfulness to Israel do for his confidence in God's actions in the future (verses 21-24)?

   What does his prayer reveal about David's attitudes toward the LORD?

8. When we find it difficult to accept a change in [the] plans we have conceived from a desire to serve the LORD, what may this reveal about our motives?

9. What do you learn from David about how to respond when God's plans involve a total change from your own?

If you've had such an experience, share it if you like with the group.

SUMMARY

1. What wonderful promises does the LORD make to David concerning?
    the people of Israel
    David himself
    David's immediate successor
    the house of God
    David's line

2. David wants to build a house for God, but God says *no,* that he intends to build David a house and kingdom that will be established forever. As you look at what David asks and what God answers, which is the greater privilege to have?

3. Judging by the choices you have been making in your life, which would you have chosen in David's place?

Conclusion

David now rules over Judah and Israel from his royal city of Jerusalem. The LORD refuses David's offer to build him a house to dwell in. His intention is for David to shepherd his people as the LORD gives them a home of their own, at rest from their enemies. Overwhelmed by the promise to build him an eternal house, David worships the LORD, asking him to keep this promise forever. David recognizes that such pledges to him and his descendants will fulfill God's covenant promises to his people Israel, and will cause other nations to praise the LORD.

Prayer

O LORD, the God of David, you are our light and our salvation, the stronghold of our life. Whom then shall we fear? You are more powerful than any enemy. Help us in the day of trouble. Keep us safe in your presence. Teach us your way. Show us where we are to go and what we are to do in these troubled times, these dangerous days. Be our shepherd and our deliverer, we pray. We ask these things for your glory, and for our good. Amen.

To prepare for Discussion 9, review briefly from Discussions 1-8 what you have learned about David's character, his skills and abilities, his relationship to God. Then read all of 2 Samuel 11 before you begin to study it using the guide questions.

DISCUSSION 9

Adultery and Murder

2 SAMUEL 7

David has consolidated his power in a series of military victories, completing the conquest begun by Joshua four hundred years earlier when the Israelites entered the Promised Land. David has broken the power of the Philistines, and they are no longer a constant threat to Israel. Now king over Judah and all the tribes of Israel, he has made Jerusalem his royal residence, *the city of David.*

Politically and geographically, Jerusalem serves to unite David's kingdom that extends from the borders of Egypt in the south to the Euphrates in the north, the same borders of the land promised to Abram in Genesis 15:18-21. By bringing the ark of God into Jerusalem, David has acknowledged that he rules under God, that the LORD is king over him and people of Israel.

When leaders publicly declare their allegiance to God, what sorts of behavior do you expect from them?

Review what you have learned about David from previous discussions. Summarize the qualities of his character, his skills and abilities, his relationship to God. Then read the full text of 2 Samuel 11 before you begin to study 1 using the guide questions.

READ 2 SAMUEL 11:1-5

1. How does David happen to get involved with Bathsheba? Compare verses 1, 11.

Note: A king did not always go out with his army if he had a competent general to head the military campaign and there were pressing duties of state at home.

2. Even after he learns Bathsheba's identity, what does David do?

3. What must be David's feelings when he receives the message in verse 5?

   What fears would arise? See also Leviticus 20:10.

READ 2 SAMUEL 11:6-13

4. What action does David proceed to take and why?

   Why does David's plan fail?

Note: For more on the kind of warrior Uriah is, see 2 Samuel 23:20-39.

5. What thoughts must cross David's mind when Uriah says what he does in verse 11?

   How does David compare with Uriah throughout this incident?

6. What new attempt does David make in verses 12, 13, to escape responsibility for his adultery?

7. Compare David's action with the warning and promise in 1 John 1:8, 9.

   If there is a matter you need to confess to the LORD to receive his forgiveness, you may wish to take time now to do it in silence.

READ 2 SAMUEL 11:14-27

8. What is the final act of David's spiritual decline?

9. What is it costing David as a person and as the king to murder Uriah?

10. Suggest a similar pattern of actions that one might find himself/herself following today in trying to cover up a sin.

11. Note the ways in which man and God view the same act of sin (verse 27). David seems to have gotten away with it, apparently forgetting all about God.

12. What steps can you take to avoid following David's pattern of action in this chapter?

    If you have followed his pattern already in some way, what steps can you take to remedy the situation?

SUMMARY

1. Contrast the David you see in this study with David in 2 Samuel, Chapter 7.

2. What do you learn about David from these two incidents?

3. How can a man guilty of the acts described in 11:1-27 be called *a man after God's own heart?*

Conclusion

At the height of his success, David falls into a network of sin that has dire consequences the rest of his life. **So if you think that you are standing firm, be careful that you don't fall!** (1 Corinthians 10:12)

Prayer

We come to you, God and Father of our LORD Jesus Christ, asking your mercy. We have indulged our physical appetites, allowed our minds to follow impure imaginations, and failed to heed your word and your will. We have accepted your gifts but often have used them selfishly, carelessly, even rebelliously. Cleanse us and forgive us, we pray, for the sake of your Son who died to free us from our sins. Amen.

In preparation for Discussion 10 during the coming week, read 2 Samuel 11, 12; Psalm 51. Then study the discussion sections using the guide questions.

DISCUSSION 10

Judgment

2 SAMUEL 12:1-25; PSALM 51

King David is at the zenith of his power in a time of relative peace when he commits adultery with Bathsheba and has her husband Uriah murdered. By these deeds, David behaves as one who has completely forgotten that he rules under God over the people of Israel. Unlike despotic rulers of other nations who may abuse their powers, David is responsible before the LORD as shepherd of his people.

At some time you may have had to confront a friend, coworker, or family member regarding wrongs that person committed. Without recounting the wrongs, how did his or her responses to you vary? How do you account for the differences in these responses?

In your preparation for this study, read the full text of 2 Samuel, chapters 11 and 12, and Psalm 51. Then study the discussion sections using the guide questions.

READ 2 SAMUEL 12:1-14

1. What is David's reaction to the story Nathan tells him (verses 1-6)?

Does David see any connection between this story and his own situation?

2. Why is this stern attitude toward the sin of others frequently characteristic of a transgressor?

   In what situations have you recognized this in yourself or in others?

3. What is the basic issue in the story Nathan tells, and in David's acts of murder and adultery?

   When Nathan directly accuses David, of what things does he specifically remind him?

   How does God view what David has done (verse 9)?

4. What will be the consequences of David's sin (verses 10–14)?

   Why can't the sinner control the results of sin?

5. How does David react to the words of the LORD through Nathan?

What does David understand about the nature of his sin?

6. Compare David's frank admission of his guilt with Saul's response to the prophet Samuel in 1 Samuel 15:17–21.

   When faced with the fact of your own sin in a specific situation, do you act more like Saul or like David?

7. When David confesses his sin (verse 13), God forgives his sin and releases him from the penalty of death for adultery and murder (Leviticus 20:10; 24:17–21). What reason does the LORD give that the child just born to David and Bathsheba will die?

READ 2 SAMUEL 12:15–25

8. What does David do during the week that the baby is so ill (verse 16, 17)?

   How does he explain his change of behavior upon the child's death?

9. How would Solomon's birth and God's message at his birth comfort David and Bathsheba?

READ PSALM 51

10. In verses 1-9, what different words does David use to describe:

    his sin

    attributes of God

    what he asks God to do

    the results (verses 7, 8)

11. Though he has sinned against Bathsheba and Uriah, David states clearly the basic issue in regard to his sin (verse 4; 2 Samuel 12:13). What does David understand that God really wants (verses 6, 16, 17)?

12. Realizing this, what does David ask God to do *in* him and *for* him (verses 7, 10, 12, 14, 15)?

SUMMARY

1. What does David do when the full impact of his sin dawns upon him?

    What then becomes David's chief concern?

2. What have you learned in today's study about God, and about what God wants of us?

CONCLUSION

The true greatness of David is *not* that he never sinned, *but* that he comes to see his sin from God's point of view, as a sin against God, a rebellion against God's holiness and righteous purposes. In Psalm 51 David acknowledges the terrible danger that sin is to a human being—not repented of, it cuts one off from fellowship with God who is the very source of life. In the contest with Goliath, David acknowledged himself dependent upon the LORD for victory over the powerful giant warrior. Now, after his sins of adultery and murder, David knows himself to be weak in every area of life, dependent upon God for all victories—moral, physical, and spiritual.

PRAYER

Gracious God, we ask you in your great mercy to blot out our misdeeds and cleanse us from our sins. Grant us humility of heart, and wisdom in our inner being. Create in us a pure heart. Give us a steadfast spirit, ready and willing to do what pleases you. Let your joy so permeate our lives that what we say and do brings honor and praise to you. We ask these things for the sake of your Son, who on the cross took our sin that we might be forgiven, and bore our separation from you that we might live in your presence. Amen.

During the next week read 2 Samuel, chapters 13 through 24. Then study the discussion sections using the guide questions for Discussion 11.

DISCUSSION 11

Reaping Consequences

2 SAMUEL 13; 15; 16; 18:1-19:1-8

When confronted about his acts of adultery and murder, David confessed his sin, and the LORD forgave him. Although David and Bathsheba are not to die for these sins, the son born to them will die, and calamities will come upon David's family and his kingdom.

Recall a lesson you learned "the hard way" in which you suffered the consequences of your actions.

As background for this study, read carefully the full text of 2 Samuel, chapters 12—24. Then study the sections for discussion using the guide questions.

1. **"You despised me and took the wife of Uriah the Hittite to be your own."** Review the specific judgments Nathan has predicted for David (12:9-14).

Read 2 Samuel 13:1, 2, 6-14, 19-20, 32-33, 37-39

2. What dreadful events take place within David's family?

3. Though David is furious when he learns about Amnon's rape of Tamar, he does nothing about the situation. How would David's own history of adultery and murder have influenced the actions of Amnon and Absalom, and affect his ability to deal justly with either son?

4. Because David fails to discipline Amnon, what action does Tamar's brother Absalom plan?

   As a result, what double loss does David suffer (13:33, 34, 38, 39)?

5. If someone under your authority or influence needs to be confronted about a wrong that person has committed, what steps can you take to work toward justice and the restoration of healthy relationships?

2 Samuel 14:23—15:7 *When David allows Absalom to return from his three-year exile, he does not see his son and restore him to his position at court for two years. Absalom is angry, for this refusal states that the king does not recognize him as his successor. Absalom shows no repentance for*

murdering his brother, and David fails to [does not] confront him personally on the issues between them. Absalom sets out to make himself widely known among the people with his chariot and horses, and bodyguard of fifty men. Over the next four years, he intercepts people coming to the king for justice, and steals their hearts. Absalom sets in motion a growing conspiracy against his father, fulfilling Nathan's prediction of calamity upon David out of his own household.

READ 2 SAMUEL 15:7-37

6. What would make Absalom's rebellion especially painful to David (15:7-12)?

   For David's reactions to someone like Ahithophel joining Absalom, see Psalm 55:12-14.

   What help is available to us at such times? See Psalm 55:1, 2a, 22, 23c; 118:6, 7a; 1 Peter 5:5b, 6, 7.

7. Describe the departure of David, his officials and his household from Jerusalem.

   In this situation, what would the steadfast loyalty of the Philistine soldiers in his personal military force (verses 18-22) mean to David?

What is the reaction of the countryside as they pass by (verse 23)?

Note: The covered head was a sign of sorrow, and to go barefoot a sign of mourning.

8. The priests and Levites carrying the ark of God accompany David as he leaves Jerusalem, but he knows that having the ark with him does not guarantee God's blessing. What is David's reasoning as he sends the ark back into the city (verses 25, 26)?

9. How is David's prayer of verse 31 answered (verses 32-37)?

READ 2 SAMUEL 16:5-15, 20-22

10. As he flees the rebellion of Absalom, what added humiliation comes upon David?

11. Absalom's actions in 16: 21, 22 indicate that he is assuming royal power, and the break between him and his father David is permanent. Compare with Nathan's prediction in 12:11, 12.

READ 2 SAMUEL 18:1-17, 32, 33; 19:1-8

12. What do you observe here about David's skills as a soldier, and how his men feel about him?

In spite of David's orders, what happens to Absalom?

While Absalom's own actions certainly have contributed to his death, David recognizes that his murder of Uriah produced the situations that led to his son's rebellion. What light does this shed on what David says and does in 18:33?

13. When David listens to Joab's rebuke of his continued mourning, what danger is avoided?

What insights do the events of 19:1-8 give you about David?

SUMMARY

1. How do David's failure to act justly in the matter of Amnon and Tamar and his laxity toward Absalom, lead to the tragedies predicted by Nathan?

2. In the midst of all the tragic events in today's study, what evidence do you see of David's trust in the LORD, and David's concern for his people?

Conclusion

The continuing consequences of David's actions toward Bathsheba and Uriah have erupted in Absalom's rebellion. The flight of David and his court from Jerusalem is a scene of deep sorrow and humiliation. When David's army engages the followers of Absalom there are very heavy casualties, and Absalom is killed. Though his army is victorious, David's personal grief over his rebellious son's death disheartens his followers, and threatens their continuing loyalty and the unity of Israel and Judah. Recognizing this, David heeds Joab's rebuke and goes out to encourage his men.

Prayer

LORD God, when we look at David's life, we see the spreading consequences of his actions toward Bathsheba and Uriah. We see how these sins influence the moral lives of his children and damage the effectiveness of his government, the morale of his army, the safety of his kingdom. Awaken us to how our thoughts and actions affect others. Deliver us from repeating David's sins. Grant that we learn to live in obedience to your commands. For our good, we pray, and for the honor of your Name. Amen.

In preparation for Discussion 12, read 2 Samuel 24; 1 Chronicles 21; 22; 28. Then study the sections listed for discussion using the guide questions.

DISCUSSION 12

Judgment and Deliverance

2 SAMUEL 24; 1 CHRONICLES 21; 22; 28

With Absalom's death, the rebellion against David's rule has ended. The men of Israel have joined with the men of Judah to bring David back to Jerusalem as king. The events of 2 Samuel 24 take place shortly after the events of 2 Samuel 15—20.

In preparation for this discussion, read 2 Samuel 24 and 1 Chronicles 21, noting the added bits of information in chapter 21. Read 1 Chronicles 22—28. Then study the sections listed for discussion using the guide questions.

READ 2 SAMUEL 24:1-10

1. There is no obvious military threat at this time (verses 1, 2). For what reasons then do you think David might want a census of all the fighting men of Israel and Judah?

    Describe Joab's opposition to such a census.

Note: **Dan to Beersheba**—*from Dan in the far north to Beersheba in the far south, the census is to include the entire land.*

2. As soon as David receives the census report almost ten months later, what does he realize (verse 10)?

READ 2 SAMUEL 24:11-17

3. In his prayer, what responsibility does David confess (verses 10,17)?

4. What characteristics of true leadership does David's prayer reveal?

   What would an analysis of your prayers show about you?

5. Of the options the LORD offers the king, which does David choose, and why?

READ 1 CHRONICLES 21:14-17

6. How severe is the plague in the land?

   At what point does the LORD stay his judgment (verses 15-17)?

READ 1 CHRONICLES 21:18-30; 22:1

7. Describe what happens at Araunah's threshing site.

   What is the significance of this site in Israel's future (1 Chronicles 22:1, and 2 Chronicles 3:1,2)?

8. In refusing Araunah's offer, what two things does David teach us about sacrifice to God (verse 24)?

9. How do many of us today exhibit the opposite concept of service to God?

   What does this reveal about our concept of God?

   about our concept of our relationship to God?

Note: Mount Moriah was the traditional site where Abraham was commanded to sacrifice Isaac (Genesis 22:2).

READ 1 CHRONICLES 22:2-19; 28:19-21

10. In his preparations for building the house of God, what materials does David provide, and what skilled workers does he arrange for (22: 2-4, 14-16)?

11. At this point, Solomon is likely about 19 years old. What reasons does David give for making such preparations for the house to be built for the LORD (verse 5)?

12. Why is Solomon to build this house, and not David (verses 6-10)?

What promises does the LORD make to David concerning Solomon, and what does David pray for his son (verses 9-12)?

13. What commands and assurances does David give to Solomon (22:13,16b; 28:9, 10, 20, 21)?

To the leaders of Israel (22: 17-19; 28:8)?

SUMMARY

1. What do you learn about David from his response to God's judgment on the people because of his own sin in ordering the census?

2. What abilities does David reveal:
    in his provisions for the temple Solomon is to build

in arrangements for the administration of the temple (see 1 Chronicles 23-26)

in arrangements for its worship services (See 1 Chronicles 23-26)

3. What do you learn about David's primary concern in all the preparations for the temple, and in his instructions to his son Solomon?

4. If there is a characteristic David exhibits in this discussion that you would like to emulate, what steps can you take to do so?

Conclusion

Today's study reveals more of David's character and the wide scope of his abilities. His concerns as king include the duties of officials and judges over Israel, and the rotation of army divisions during the year. When his insistence on a census of Israel's fighting men brings the judgment of a plague, David takes responsibility for his actions and intercedes for his people. The LORD answers his prayers. The plague is stopped, and Araunah's threshing floor where God accepts David's offerings becomes the place where the house of the LORD God is to be built.

David reveals a sensitive repentant heart toward God, a tender concern for his people, and a deep desire that the leaders of Israel and his son Solomon will serve the LORD with a whole heart and a willing mind. He intends the temple that Solomon builds shall bring honor to the LORD before all nations. To this end, David concentrates his administrative skills and abilities in preparations for the temple whose plans the LORD has put in his mind.

PRAYER

O God, in coming to you we realize that we come to the One who is the LORD, the God of David. As we study your servant David, we want to learn from him what it means to please you, to serve you with all the abilities you have given us. Open our eyes to the responsibilities you have given us in our families, our neighborhoods and our communities. Grant each of us increasing sensitivity to your desires and your concerns. Show us how to love you with a whole heart. May you be honored in every part of our lives. For the sake of your great name, we pray. Amen.

In preparation for Discussion 13, study Psalm 71 using the guide questions. Then review your discoveries of David's life and character and the applications to your own life in Discussions 1-12.

DISCUSSION 13

Review of the Life of David

PSALM 71

During the week preceding this discussion, study Psalm 71, and review your discoveries in Discussions 1-12. As you refer to your notes, summarize what you learned about David. Note particularly what you learned about:

> *the basic commitment of David's life*
> *attitudes and actions to emulate*
> *mistakes to avoid*
> *honesty before God*
> *developing a living, growing relationship with God*

If Psalm 70 is viewed as an introduction to Psalm 71, then this psalm speaks of David's concerns in his old age. **Allot 30 minutes to discuss Psalm 71 using the questions provided.**

READ PSALM 71 ALOUD

1. By what names does David address the LORD (verses 1, 4, 5, 12, 16, 22)?

2. What do you learn about God, and what he has done for David, from the descriptive words and phrases that the psalmist uses?

   Which of these describe ways in which you have experienced God?

3. What does David ask God to do for him (verses 1-4, 9, 12, 18)?

4. In response to God's actions, what does the psalmist do (verse 8) and promise to do (verses 14-16, 22-24)?

   How may doing such things help you when you are weak, discouraged or threatened?

5. What does David use to express his worship of the LORD (verses 22-24)?

   Which of these means do you use to worship God?

After discussing Psalm 71, discuss the following Review questions:

1. How do Discussions 1-12 confirm Samuel's words that David would be the kind of man God wants, **a man after his own heart** (1 Samuel 13:14)?

2. What is the basic commitment of David's life to which he always returns?

3. How does this basic commitment of David's life affect his actions as:
    a youth fighting against Goliath

    a fugitive from the king's jealous wrath

    a powerful monarch with a kingdom at peace

    a sinner against man and God when faced with his crimes

    a king facing the terrible consequences of his own sin in his family and kingdom

    a king preparing to pass the kingdom to his young son

4. What words or actions reveal that David values what God values?

5. What do you learn from David' sins and failures?

6. What episode in David's life is most striking to you? Why?

7. In what one area do you most want to emulate David?

   What steps can you take to do this?

CONCLUSION

In this series of discussions, you have met David:
- a keeper of sheep who became God's shepherd of a nation

- the poet musician whose psalms are prayed and sung today

- a warrior leader who extended the united Judah and Israel from the borders of Sinai to the River Euphrates

- a man passionate in his growing relationship with God from youth to old age

- a repentant sinner who recognized and confessed his sin against God but whose acts brought terrible results in his family and nation

- the ruler whom God promised that his throne would be established forever

PRAYER

Gracious God, Grant us the kind of confidence in you that David had. Deliver us from evil and cruel enemies. Deliver us also from trusting in our own might and wisdom. Lead us into a deepening relationship with you through ordinary days, and in times of stress and difficulty.

We ask for courage to be honest before you. Deliver us from rationalizing sin or evading responsibility for it. Forgive us for the sake of your Son who bore our sins in his own body on the cross.

Help us to learn from the mistakes David made in his family relationships. Teach us to love and serve our families, our friends, our neighbors, our community and nation. Enable us to use the talents and abilities you have given us to serve you with joy in our generation as David served you in his. We pray in the name of Jesus Christ, the Son of David. Amen.

WHAT SHOULD OUR GROUP STUDY NEXT?

We recommend the Gospel of Mark, the fast paced narrative of Jesus' life, as the first book for people new to Bible study. Follow this with the Book of Acts to see what happens to the people introduced in Mark. Then in Genesis discover the beginnings of the world and find the answers to the big questions of where we came from and why we are here.

Our repertoire of guides allows great flexibility. For groups starting with *Lenten Studies, They Met Jesus* is a good sequel.

LEVEL 101: little or no previous Bible study experience

Mark (recommended first unit of study) or The Book of Mark (Simplified English)
Acts, Books 1 and 2
Genesis, Books 1 and 2
Psalms/Proverbs
Topical Studies
Conversations With Jesus
Lenten Studies
Foundations for Faith
Character Studies
They Met Jesus

> **Sequence for groups reaching people from non-Christian cultures**
> Foundations for Faith
> Genesis, Books 1 and 2
> Mark, Discover Jesus *or* The Book of Mark
> *(Simplified English)*

LEVEL 201: some experience in Bible study (after 3-4 Level 101 books)

John, Books 1 and 2
Romans
Luke
I John/James
1 Corinthians
2 Corinthians
Philippians
Colossians
Topical Studies
Prayer
Treasures
Relationships
Servants of the Lord
Work - God's Gift
Celebrate
Character Studies
Four Men of God
Lifestyles of Faith, Books 1 and 2

LEVEL 301: More experienced in Bible study

Matthew, Books 1 and 2
Galatians & Philemon
1 and 2 Peter
Hebrews
1 and 2 Thessalonians, 2 & 3 John
Isaiah
Ephesians
Topical Studies
Set Free
Character Studies
Moses
David
***Biweekly or Monthly Groups may use topical studies of character studies.*

ABOUT NEIGHBORHOOD BIBLE STUDIES

Neighborhood Bible Studies, Inc. is a leader in the field of small group Bible studies. Since 1960, NBS has pioneered the development of Bible study groups that encourage each member to participate in the leadership of the discussion.

The mission of Neighborhood Bible Studies is to: Mobilize and empower followers of Jesus Christ to introduce and multiply small group discussion Bible studies among their neighbors, co-workers, and friends so that participants can encounter God, grow in faith, and pattern their lives after Jesus.

The vision of Neighborhood Bible Studies is to: Invite people everywhere to a relationship with Christ through the study of God's word.

Publication in more than 20 languages indicates the versatility of NBS cross culturally. NBS **methods and materials** are used around the world to:

> Equip individuals for facilitating discovery Bible studies
> Serve as a resource to the church

Skilled NBS personnel provide consultation by telephone or e-mail. In some areas, they conduct workshops and seminars to train individuals, clergy, and laity in how to establish small group Bible studies in neighborhoods, churches, workplaces and specialized facilities. **Call 1-800-369-0307 to inquire about consultation or training.**

ABOUT THE FOUNDERS

Marilyn Kunz and Catherine Schell, authors of many of the NBS guides, founded Neighborhood Bible Studies and directed its work for thirty-one years. Currently other authors contribute to the series.

The cost of your study guide has been subsidized by faithful people who give generously to NBS. For more information, visit our web site: www.neighborhoodbiblestudy.org *1-800-369-0307*

COMPLETE LISTING OF NBS STUDY GUIDES

Getting Started
How to Start a Neighborhood Bible Study (*handbook & video or audio cassette*)

Bible Book Studies
Genesis, Book 1 *Begin with God*
Genesis, Book 2 *Discover Your Roots*
Psalms & Proverbs *Journals of Wisdom*
Isaiah *God's Help Is on the Way*
Matthew, Book 1 *God's Promise Kept*
Matthew, Book 2 *God's Purpose Fulfilled*
Mark *Discover Jesus*
Luke *Good News and Great Joy*
John, Book 1 *Explore Faith and Understand Life*
John, Book 2 *Believe and Live*
Acts, Book 1 *The Holy Spirit Transforms Lives*
Acts, Book 2 *Amazing Journeys with God*
Romans *A Reasoned Faith*
1 Corinthians *Finding Answers to Life's Questions*
2 Corinthians *The Power of Weakness*
Galatians & Philemon *Fully Accepted by God*
Ephesians *Living in God's Family*
Philippians *A Message of Encouragement*
Colossians *Staying Focused on Truth*
1 & 2 Thessalonians, 2 & 3 John, Jude *The Coming of the LORD*
Hebrews *Access to God*
1 & 2 Peter *Strength Amidst Stress*
1 John & James *Faith that Lives*

Topical Studies
Celebrate *Reasons for Hurrahs*
Conversations with Jesus *Getting to Know Him*
Change *Facing the Unexpected*
Foundations for Faith *The Basics for Knowing God*
Lenten Studies *Life Defeats Death*
Prayer *Communicating with God*
Relationships *Connect to Others: God's Plan*
Servants of the LORD *Embrace God's Agenda*
Set Free *Leaving Negative Emotions Behind*
Treasures *Discover God's Riches*
Work - God's Gift *Life-Changing Choices*

Character Studies
Four Men of God *Unlikely Leaders*
Lifestyles of Faith, Book One *Choosing to Trust God*
Lifestyles of Faith, Book Two *Choosing to Obey God*
They Met Jesus *Life-Changing Encounters*
David *Passion Pursued*
Moses *Learning to Lead*

Simplified English
The Book of Mark *The Story of Jesus*